Praise for *Green Flags*

"Autrey's *Green Flags* is a probing, thoughtful introduction to the dynamics of relationships and will go a long way toward helping us understand why relationships so often turn out the way they do, and why something we say is so desirable is often so complicated. But be warned, this book will ask the reader to have the courage to look within to examine our relationship to our own lives, for we are the only person who is common to all of our relationships. It only seems common sense, then, that to improve outer relationships, we have to learn much more about that person we are bringing to all our engagements with others."

–James Hollis, PhD, Jungian analyst and author in Washington, D.C.

"It is rare that one comes across a book that is so easy to read, but also so profound. In his book, *Green Flags*, Quique Autrey provides his readers with an encouraging guide for becoming more effective in creating and maintaining relationships. If approached with an open mind and a willingness to look deeper into why we do the things we do, this book will enlighten and empower readers in their quest for obtaining more contentment and connection in their lives."

–Paul J. Leslie, author of *The Art of Creating a Magical Session: Key Elements for Transformative Psychotherapy*

"In my tradition, our weekly assembly begins addressing the presence of God: '...unto to whom all hearts are open, all desires known, and from whom no secrets are hid...' If God knows us so completely, then we would do well to be honest with ourselves about who we are especially when we relate to God, and those through whom we know God, our family, friends, and community. Autrey's book is a helpful and accessible tool to explore our own hearts, desires, and secrets so that we might be bearers of green flags to ourselves and our community."

–The Rev. J. James Derkits, M Div, Rector of Trinity by the Sea Episcopal Church, Port Aransas

"Throughout our lives, each of us inevitably confronts the paradox that while we journey alone, we cannot truly live on our own. We need Wayfinders to guide us through the evolving myth of our lives. *Green Flags* reveals that the path to self-discovery often lies in what we observe outside ourselves, ultimately leading us back to what we've concealed within. By recognizing this, we deepen our connection with ourselves and others, freeing them from the burdens we unconsciously project. *Green Flags* lights the way, guiding us to rediscover our truest selves."

–John Price, PhD, Co-Founder of the Center for the Healing Arts & Sciences and host of *The Sacred Speaks* podcast.

We might initially think that the person we know best is ourselves, after all that's who we spend every waking morment with. Yet it is often our own selves that we know least about. Our conscious ego—with its desires—is easy to see, but our unconscious wishes are elusive, often only showing up indirectly in our judgments of others, our inhibitions and our repetitions. Not only do we not know ourselves, but we don't know that we don't know ourselves. Add to that the fact that we have all sorts of ingenious defences set up to avoid such a knowledge and one might conclude that we will never really encounter the subject that we are. For this reason, we are in dire need of *Green Flags*. With great skill, Autrey helps the reader to identify their defences. But Autrey offers us more than his skill and insight, he demonstrates a deep compassion in his writing, a compassion that offers the reader the grace that is needed to actually lower those defences and encounter themselves. An endeavour that promises to bear fruit in self-discovery, self-transformation and in a richer engagement with others.

–Peter Rollins, radical theologian and author of *The Idolatry of God*

"I liked *Green Flags* for its insight, but I loved *Green Flags* for its humanity; that is, its ability to be gracious even as it sheds light on critical psychological concepts. I highly recommend this book. It's an important read for anyone interested in becoming the person they need to become."

–Jonathan J. Foster, PhD, author of *Indigo: The Color of Grief*

Autrey's new book *Green Flags* is an eloquent and exciting personal and practical work that tarries with profound questions related to the complex needs of the human subject, to the 'problem' of subjectivity and to the importance and difficulties of intersubjectivity and interpersonal relationships. Whilst many practical books aim at 'conscious-raising' related to these issues, Autrey's does something much more challenging and important—aiming at raising the contours of the reader's unconscious. Instead of offering neat solutions, Autrey guides his reader towards an encounter with the unconscious dynamic of their life—with all the complexity and difficulty that that entails—and does so with humor and insight. *Green Flags* is a stimulating and life-affirming text from an experienced practitioner and a brilliant writer and thinker.

–Helen Rollins, author of *Psychocinema a*nd co-host of *The Lack* podcast

"In clear and vivid terms, Autrey's book revives the great insight of Aristotle that good friendships don't happen by accident but require thoughtful effort and care to bring out the best in the friend, and in oneself."

–Richard Boothby, PhD, professor of philosophy and author of *Blown Away: Refinding Life After My Son's Suicide*

GREEN FLAGS

HOW TO BE THE KIND OF PERSON YOU NEED IN YOUR LIFE

∞ Possibilities Press

Copyright © 2024 Quique Autrey
All rights reserved
Published in the United States by Possibilies Press

All rights reserved. No part of this book may be reproduced or transmitted in any form or by any means, electronic or mechanical, including photocopying, recording, or by an information storage and retrieval system — except by a reviewer who may quote brief passages in a review to be printed in a magazine or newspaper — without permission in writing from the publisher.

To protect the privacy of certain individuals the names and identifying details have been changed.

979-8-9916143-0-6 ISBN Hardcover
979-8-9916143-1-3 ISBN Paperback
979-8-9916143-2-0 ISBN Ebook
Library of Congress Control Number: 2024920080
Printed in the United States of America
First Edition

Book design Houston Creative Space
Cover image by Valeriya Simantovskaya
Author photograph by Angi Lewis

POSSIBILITIES
PRESS

GREEN FLAGS

**HOW TO BE
THE KIND
OF PERSON
YOU NEED
IN YOUR LIFE**

Quique Autrcy

*To Amy, my best friend and soul mate.
Your love, support, and unwavering belief in me
have made all things possible. This book is as much
yours as it is mine. Thank you for being my partner
in every sense of the word. I am forever grateful to
share this journey with you.*

CONTENTS

INTRODUCTION 13

CHAPTER 1 Celebrate The Wins of Others 23

CHAPTER 2 Remember The Small Things 33

CHAPTER 3 Respect Boundaries 41

CHAPTER 4 Manage Your Anxiety 49

CHAPTER 5 Listen Without Being Defensive 57

CHAPTER 6 Let Others Be Themselves 63

CHAPTER 7 Help People Feel Safe 71

CHAPTER 8 Don't Project unto Others 79

CHAPTER 9 Support Others' Goals 85

CONCLUSION
Continuing to Bring Forth What is Within 91

ENDNOTES 93

ACKNOWLEDGEMENTS 99

ABOUT THE AUTHOR 101

INTRODUCTION

"The quality of all our relationships is a direct function of our relationship to ourselves."

–James Hollis[1]

The above quote lingers with me to this day. I encountered it on a bleak and rainy Sunday morning. Before anyone else in the house was up, I picked up Hollis' *The Eden Project: In Search of The Magical Other* and started reading.

The book was a recommendation from my therapist. At the time, I was a year into weekly therapy sessions with him. Therapy sessions started after my life and career collapsed. The year prior to starting therapy, I was a senior pastor in Colorado. This role was the culmination of a decade working in various churches. Almost a year into that position, I started an affair with a woman who was a staff member. When my infidelity was exposed, I lost my job, my marriage fell apart, and any faith I had was shattered.

Initially, therapy was an attempt to save my marriage and figure out what I was going to do for employment. It quickly became something much more than this. I established a strong connection with my therapist. He fostered a safe space to explore my deepest fears and longings. While therapy helped me discern that I needed to proceed with a divorce and take serious steps towards becoming a therapist, *the real gift of therapy was helping me come to terms with my own unhealthy relationship to myself.*

My life and relationships were a mess due to avoiding grappling with my inner demons. This is why Hollis' quote lingered in my mind so long. The life and relationships I dreamt of would not be possible unless I worked on a more honest relationship to myself.

There is a trend in our culture to point the finger and highlight everyone else's faults. Many of us are quick to label someone we do not like a narcissist or point out the "red flags" that make us uncomfortable. Sometimes this is necessary, but often *what is needed is a humble attitude that allows us to confront our own flaws rather than projecting our problems onto others.*

Stoic philosopher and Roman emperor Marcus Aurelius advised:

> Whenever you are about to find fault with someone, ask yourself the following question: What fault of mine most nearly resembles the one I am about to criticize?[2]

The modern author Ryan Holiday paraphrases this

ancient advice with the following maxim, "Be tolerant with others and strict with yourself."[3] This is much needed wisdom in an age tempted to blame others and not take responsibility for oneself.

THE FUNCTION OF THERAPY IS TO HELP MAKE THE UNCONSCIOUS CONSCIOUS.

My therapist embraced a depth psychological[4] approach to working with people. At its core, depth psychology acknowledges that psychic processes are partly unconscious and partly conscious. This means we all do things for reasons we are not always immediately aware of. Destructive behaviors such as, overeating or an addiction to gambling may be motivated by reasons outside a person's conscious intentions.

One of the hopes of depth psychology is that people can come to a greater awareness of what governs their behavior. One common description is that *the function of therapy is to help make the unconscious conscious.*

To do this, it will be helpful to create a roadmap toward becoming the person we want to be. This book will not only dive into the unconscious roots of our behaviors, but also focus on positive, intentional steps towards becoming the person who we need to be for both us and others.

All of us can imagine the kind of person we would

like to have in our lives, someone who listens to us, understands who we are, accepts us where we're at. But to become this kind of person, the first step is to understand why we do what we do.

The other day, I came across an *instagram* post from @herpsychology, which alerted me to a set of characteristics I wish I'd knew about twenty years ago:

Green flags in people:

- They celebrate the wins of people
- Remember the small things about you
- They respect your boundaries
- You feel energized after seeing them
- They listen without being defensive
- They allow you to be fully yourself
- They make you feel safe
- You don't have to watch what you say
- They support your goals[5]

The focus on "green flags" instead of the usual emphasis on "red flags" set this image apart from the thousands of mental health images on my *instagram* feed. Multiple therapists and influencers I follow highlight the dangers of "red flag" people and how to avoid them. It was refreshing to read a post about the virtues of someone who extols the traits and values of a healthy person whose relationships with self and others is focused on the positive behaviors and aspirations.

INTRODUCTION

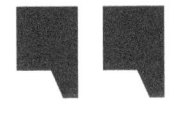

THIS BOOK IS ABOUT HELPING YOU BECOME LESS OF A BURDEN ON OTHER PEOPLE BY TEACHING YOU HOW TO DEVELOP A HEALTHIER RELATIONSHIP TO YOURSELF.

If there are such things as a "red flag" person or character traits that raise "red flags" then there must be characteristics of "green flag" people.

After reflecting on the image for some time, it dawned on me why it initially grabbed my attention. *The image reminded me of the challenging work I did in therapy to cultivate a healthier relationship with myself and others.*

When I consider "green flags," I envision someone who has examined their unconscious patterns and actively worked to resolve them, reducing the suffering they experience in their life and relationships.

People with "green flags" are not just safe; they are genuinely enjoyable to be around, and they energize others instead of draining them. My therapy journey has convinced me that becoming someone others perceive as marked by "green flags" requires a great deal of introspection, consistently challenging and examining of our unconscious patterns. Returning to the Hollis quote, a person characterized by "green flags" is one who has worked on their relationship to themselves. This is evident by how they interact with others.

My wife and I, who are both therapists, often joke that we do not really like people. After years of making this joke, I have realized this is only a half-truth. It is not that we dislike all people; what we do not like are those who drain us and unconsciously burden us with their unresolved psychological baggage. This is not limited to our clients; we have acquaintances, friends, and family members who fit this description too.

This book is about helping you become less of a burden on other people by teaching you how to develop a healthier relationship to yourself.

Each chapter will delve into one of the "green flags" featured in the *instagram* post. Each of the nine positive statements presupposes an underlying negative unconscious pattern that everyone must recognize and address to become the kind of person others find energizing and enjoyable.

Chapter one explores the truth that healthy people celebrate the wins of others. The negative unconscious pattern that must be worked on is our tendency to feel insecure when others are thriving.

Chapter two emphasizes our tendency to connect with aspects of others that are exciting and fulfill our narcissistic needs. While not inherently problematic, if this becomes the main reason for relating to

INTRODUCTION

someone, we overlook the ordinary aspects that truly define them. If you have ever been frustrated by someone who only wants to spend time with you for what you can do for them, you will understand exactly what I mean.

Chapter three explains that we will only respect the boundaries of other people when we respect our own boundaries. Getting clear about boundaries requires that we understand why it is hard to establish them and reinforce them with others. When we have the tools to create healthy boundaries, we better understand how to honor the boundaries of others.

Chapter four asserts that when we are around healthy people, we tend to feel energized rather than depleted. This is because unhealthy people tend to unconsciously project their anxieties. If we can learn to manage our underlying anxiety, we can relate to others without burdening them with something that is not theirs to carry.

Chapter five reveals that healthy individuals listen without becoming defensive. The negative unconscious pattern to address is our natural tendency to identify with our beliefs, which can lead to taking things personally.

Chapter six explores the importance of confidence in a relationship. Unhealthy individuals struggle to let others be their true selves because it threatens their own sense of identity. As we build confidence by self-acceptance, we can interact with others in a way that affirms their authenticity without feeling the need to change ourselves.

Chapter seven argues that healthy people behave in a way that leads to greater trust in a relationship. Unhealthy individuals consciously and unconsciously deceive themselves and others about their true intentions. When this happens, people feel unsafe, and relationships fall apart.

Chapter eight addresses the importance of adopting a non-judgmental attitude in our relationship to other people. Unhealthy individuals are too easily offended by what others say and believe. Learning to accept people even when we disagree with their behavior or values is not only possible but essential to quality relationships.

Chapter nine examines the importance of supporting others' goals. Healthy individuals approach relationships with a spirit of collaboration rather than competition. This does not mean that all competition is bad; there can be healthy competition within a broader context of mutual support and affirmation. Healthy people support others' dreams because they recognize the benefits of reciprocal support.

Throughout the book I will share personal stories and examples from clients and other people in my life to help illustrate the points I want to make. While all of these have a kernel of truth to them, I have intentionally changed the names and some of the details to protect each individual's confidential-

INTRODUCTION

ity.

Each chapter ends with a set of discussion questions and tools for practice. The questions are intended to help you further process the content of each chapter. The tools are to provide actionable suggestions. These questions would be great to discuss with a friend, partner, or therapist—any trusted person in your life who is courageous enough to speak the truth to you in love.

No one person perfectly embodies the virtues of a healthy person described in this book, including myself. While I have grown and matured tremendously over the last twenty years, I am still a work in progress. The unhealthy unconscious patterns that I explore in these pages are something I struggle with daily. The important thing is that I am more aware of my flaws, and I actively seek to address them for the sake of my relationship to myself and others.

One of the central assumptions of depth psychology is that we cannot see our deeply ingrained unconscious patterns all by ourselves. This is why we need therapists, spouses, and friends to help us see our blind spots. As you read this book, *I encourage you to discuss it with someone who can see what you cannot see*. I am not suggesting this person needs to be a therapist (although that can be very helpful). It can be any trusted person in your life who is courageous enough to speak the truth to you in love.

NOTES

CHAPTER 1

Celebrate The Wins of Others

"Promise yourself today to be just as enthusiastic about the success of others as you are about your own."

–Christian D. Larson[1]

"Green flag" individuals celebrate the wins of other people in their life. I know, much easier said than done! This can be such a challenge because many of us have not adequately grappled with feelings of shame, inadequacy and low self-esteem. *Our underlying insecurities can prevent us from affirming and celebrating the good fortune and successes of others, unless we address our underlying insecurities.*

This has been a struggle throughout my life. In my childhood, I battled intense feelings of inadequacy. My best theory is these feelings emerged from several sources. I grew up in a tumultuous home with a father who was diagnosed with bipolar disorder. In 5th grade, I was diagnosed with Tourette Syndrome. To this day, there is still uncertainty as to how much this diagnosis was rooted in neurological differences and how much of it was my body's reaction to early traumatic experiences.

Starting in junior high, weight and body image

were a battle. Even though I was tall, I eventually reached a size of over three hundred pounds. My older brothers and multiple people at school bullied me because of my obesity and the strange tics and noises stemming from Tourette's.

The combination of an unstable relationship with my father, a socially debilitating diagnosis, and years of bullying led me to develop a persistent sense of shame and inadequacy. I felt inferior to other people and had little to no social status.

In my late teens, I converted to Christianity. I was drawn to my friend's family, who seemed more present and affectionate than my own. Eventually, they invited me to Lakewood Church, in Houston, Texas, and I was compelled by Joel Osteen's message of hope and positivity.

With this turn to religion, I mustered up enough willpower to start exercising and adopted a more reasonable diet. In the span of a year, I lost a hundred pounds. I was going to college and working part-time. For the first time in my life, I felt decent about my appearance and found social status through the church. People started recognizing me for my strengths and abilities rather than emphasizing my deficiencies.

As significant as these changes were, I was *not really addressing the deep-seated feelings of shame and inadequacy.*

No matter how well I was doing, I could not help

CHAPTER 1

but become upset by the accomplishments and good fortune of my friends and family. If a classmate excelled at a presentation, I would publicly congratulate them while internally criticizing them. It came to the point where I refused to attend events where friends were being celebrated because I did not want to be flooded by feelings of inferiority.

In my mid-twenties, I worked as a youth pastor in a small church plant. My friend Tim was a fellow pastor of a church close to the one where I worked. During one of our frequent coffee outings, he paused our conversation and asked me what was wrong. I was initially taken aback. I was not sure what he was referring to.

Tim was brave and confident enough to ask: "You're always making faces and squirming in your seat when I talk about the things that are going well in my congregation. Is there something you need to talk about?"

I was speechless, and did not know how to respond. Honestly, I was oblivious to my non-verbal reactions and ignorant of the root of the behavior. Sadly, my relationship with Tim fizzled out. We never talked about why the relationship fell apart, but my guess is Tim got fed up with my insecurities. I wasn't courageous yet to delve into my insecurities and communicate them to Tim.

In therapy sessions, clients frequently struggle with these feelings of inadequacy. Recently, a client named Georgia came to see me. She wanted help transitioning out of her final year of college and into the workforce. She was also looking for a way to understand her recent bouts of anger.

Georgia was diagnosed with autism spectrum disorder (ASD)[2] as a young child. She revealed that she was the oldest of two girls and that her younger sister was neurotypical.[3] Georgia found herself getting upset with her sister every time she was around her. Georgia struggled making friends and was taking longer than planned to learn how to drive. Her sister, who was still in high school, had lots of friends and drove confidently. As patient and loving as her sister was, she started to distance herself when Georgia begun calling her names and losing her temper. After talking in therapy, we discovered Georgia was getting so upset because her sisters' apparent "normalcy" was bringing up feelings of shame and inadequacy. The recent anger outbursts were a reaction to her deep-seated sense of inferiority.

Georgia was motivated to work on her inferiority because it was taking a toll on her relationship with her sister. Her sister adored Georgia very much and was very patient with her neurodivergence. However, Georgia's recent anger outbursts were very hurtful to her sister. Georgia would call her sister names and make demeaning comments anytime her sense of inadequacy was triggered. She was afraid that she would ruin her relationship with her sister if she did not get this under control.

CHAPTER 1

In *The Road Less Traveled*, psychiatrist M. Scott Peck states, "We cannot solve a problem by hoping someone else will solve it for us. I can solve a problem only when I say, 'This is my problem and it's up to me to solve it.'"[4]

> **OUR UNDERLYING INSECURITIES CAN PREVENT US FROM AFFIRMING AND CELEBRATING THE GOOD FORTUNE AND SUCCESSES OF OTHERS, UNLESS WE ADDRESS OUR UNDERLYING INSECURITIES.**

Here, Peck is calling us to take responsibility for our own deep-seated issues. This is not to suggest that our diagnoses or traumas are our fault. They are not, but if *we hope to make any progress in becoming a healthy person people want to be around, we must accept our psychological baggage and do something to address it.*

It took me years in a therapist's chair to finally uncover and address my entrenched sense of shame and low self-esteem. I had to learn to accept my past and find a way to value myself before I could hope to be in a healthy relationship with anyone else. Once I could do this, I was not so threatened by the successes of friends, family and co-workers. When I started to believe in my own worth and dignity, I could easily celebrate the wins of others.

The same thing happened with Georgia. She was understandably frustrated that her parents were not allowing her to drive. To their credit, her slower processing and tendency to get overwhelmed and distracted made driving a real challenge and potential hazard to herself and others.

We decided one of the only ways she was going to feel "normal" was by learning how to drive. We worked together and found a driving program that worked specifically with Autistic people. After a few months, she passed the driving test and received her license. Georgia's esteem was greatly boosted by being able to drive herself to therapy. Although she still gets irritated with her sister, she no longer has the uncontrollable anger outbursts.

Shame and inadequacy no longer have such a strong hold over me and my relationships. This has very little to do with external accomplishments and much more to do with self-love and acceptance. One of the great things about addressing my shame is my increased ability to celebrate my friends and family when they experience success. Instead of avoiding triggering situations, I now look for opportunities to praise loved ones for their good fortune.

CHAPTER 1

Tools for Practice

> **Brené Brown offers the following definition of shame:**
>
> "Shame is the intensely painful feeling or experience of believing that we are flawed and therefore unworthy of love, belonging, and connection."[5]
>
> One of the most effective ways to counter the power of shame is by practicing self-compassion. Self-compassion has three important elements.

Managing Shame Through Self-Compassion[6]

1. Self-Kindness over Self-Judgement

Practicing self-kindness means becoming more empathetic and gentler with ourselves when we perceive our flaws and imperfections.

The next time you are overwhelmed with feelings of shame, imagine that your best friend is going through the same situation you are.

How would you talk them through their negative feelings? Now try to relate to yourself in the same spirit of kindness and understanding.

GREEN FLAGS

2. *Common Humanity over Isolation*

Shame and inadequacy are negative emotions that everyone struggles with. The great temptation when we are battling shame is believing that we are the only ones struggling with this.

Instead of isolating yourself when you are feeling shame, reach out to a friend and talk about what you are feeling.

3. *Mindfulness rather than Over-Identification*

Mindfulness is the non-judgmental awareness of an emotional or bodily state. When we practice mindfulness, we acknowledge the shame without denying it or identifying with it.

The mind is like a train station. Our negative thoughts and emotions are trains that come in and out of the station. Like a traveler at the station, we cannot control the trains coming in and out of the station. What we do have some control over is whether we get on the train. Likewise, we cannot control when thoughts and feelings around shame come into our awareness. We do, however, have some agency over whether we identify and perpetuate those negative thoughts and feelings.

Take a few minutes a day to practice this mindfulness exercise:

Imagine your negative thoughts and feelings as

CHAPTER 1

trains at a station. Without judging them, notice them and watch them pass through the station. Try not to get on the trains when they arrive. If negative thoughts and emotions arise, change the way you relate to them. Remember, you are not your thoughts or emotions.

Questions For Discussion

1. Is it difficult for you to celebrate the wins of others? If so, why?

_____
_____
_____
_____
_____
_____

2. Are you aware of any insecurities that might be blocking you from praising others?

_____
_____
_____
_____
_____

3. Think of one person in your life that's hard to celebrate. Why do you think that is?

_____
_____

GREEN FLAGS

_____
_____
_____
_____
_____

4. Who is someone in your life that needs encouragement? What is something significant you can do for them today?

_____
_____
_____
_____
_____
_____

CHAPTER 2

Remember The Small Things

"Love isn't something natural. Rather it requires discipline, concentration, patience, faith, and the overcoming of narcissism. It isn't a feeling, it is a practice."

–Erich Fromm[1]

In the quote above, psychoanalyst Erich Fromm claims true love involves the overcoming of narcissism. While most of us do not have narcissistic personality disorder (NPD)[2], we all struggle with unconscious narcissistic tendencies.

We often look to other people to secure our sense of self. Philosopher Richard Boothby puts it this way, "falling in love is a matter of unconsciously finding in the beloved a mirror that stabilizes one's own ego."[3]

When we relate to others as a way to stabilize our own sense of self, we are using them to meet our needs.

Several years ago, I formed an online friendship with a prominent figure in the psychotherapy field, someone who had gained a bit of celebrity status within our profession. He was an accomplished author and respected professor. We did a few podcast episodes together and developed an amicable connection through private messages.

At no fault of his own, my friend endured several life-altering crises that left him unemployed, seriously in debt, and at the brink of homelessness. I maintained a strong connection with him through this tumultuous season of his life.

After several months of intense suffering, my friend was able to find a stable job and a place to live. He shared with me that one of the hardest parts of going through the hellish year was realizing how few true friends he truly had. He reported that most of the people that reached out to him were only interested in his writings and fame. Their love for him was narcissistic. They were relating to a fantasy of who they wanted him to be, rather than him as an individual.

I could relate. When I was fired as senior pastor, I scrambled to find a new job back in Texas to support my family. Before all this, I had scores of people that would call me their friend. My phone was constantly buzzing with text messages. Everyone wanted a piece of me while I was the young, charismatic pastor.

When things fell apart, the text messages and attention from others withered away. It was a difficult and lonely season of my life. At one point, I remember doing a bit of an experiment. It was tiring being the one who initiated communication with people I had seen as true friends, so I decided to wait for someone to text me first. After several weeks, there was silence. Eventually, an old friend from seminary reached out and asked to hang out. To this day, he is one of the only friends from my past that I stay connected to.

> **WHEN SOMEONE REMEMBERS WHAT MIGHT BE SEEMINGLY INSIGNIFICANT, THEY ARE COMMUNICATING THEY CARE ABOUT THE PARTS OF US THAT DO NOT NECESSARILY PROP UP THEIR EGO OR FUEL THEIR FANTASIES.**

Fromm was right to highlight that authentic love is unnatural. It is unnatural not in the sense that it is completely alien to us, but in the sense that it takes conscious effort to practice it. What usually gets labeled as "love" in our society is more of the narcissistic reinforcement of the ego than something beautiful and sublime. Love calls for an authentic response.

"Green flag" people remember the small things about us. This is less about having a great memory or an attuned attention to details. It is about setting priorities and focus.

When someone remembers what might be seemingly insignificant, they are communicating they care about the parts of us that do not necessarily prop up their ego or fuel their fantasies.

It was meaningful when my online friend thanked me for being there for him through one of the darkest periods of his life. He said he appreciated me just checking in on him, asking him about his family, and taking time to let him talk about what was most relevant for him.

Having been in profoundly dark places, the memory of being loved in ordinary ways deeply inspired me to be there for my friend.

While we might never outgrow all of our narcissistic tendencies, I agree with Fromm that it is possible to grow in genuine love through discipline, concentration, patience, and faith.

Tools for Practice

Practicing Love Through Active Listening

Active listening is a model of communication that enhances understanding between people.[4] Listening without a specific agenda is one of the most effective ways to love someone. There are five key elements of active listening, each designed to ensure that you truly hear the other person.[5] These five elements are (1) pay attention, (2) show that you are listening, (3) provide feedback, (4) defer judgement, and (5) respond appropriately.

CHAPTER 2

Pick someone in your life that is going through a tough time. Make it a goal to practice these five elements when you listen to them over the next few weeks.

1. *Pay Attention*

Give the person your undivided attention. Do not mentally prepare for what you are going to say in response. A book I recommend is The Art of Listening by Michael Nichols.

2. *Show That You Are Listening*

Use body language and gestures to communicate that you are interested in what they are saying (e.g., nod on occasion). Smiling and using other facial expressions can help too. Ensure your posture is open and inviting. Encourage the person to continue by using small verbal cues like "Yes" and "Aha."

3. *Provide Feedback*

Provide feedback by reflecting and asking questions to ensure understanding. Paraphrase with phrases like "What I'm hearing is" or "Sounds like you are saying," Ask clarifying questions and periodically summarize the speaker's comments.

4. *Defer Judgement*

It is important to withhold judgment. Even if you disagree with what is being said, wait until the other person has finished before you respond. The goal of active listening is understanding, not agreement.

5. Respond Appropriately

Make sure your response is on topic. Be clear and honest while maintaining respect for the other person.

Questions for Discussion

1. Is there anyone in your life that uses you in the narcissistic way described in this chapter? If so, explore how that makes you feel.

___

___

___

___

___

___

2. Is there someone in your life that you relate to in a narcissistic way? Why do you think that is?

___

___

___

___

___

___

3. What does the quote from Erich Fromm at

CHAPTER 2

the beginning of the chapter mean for you?

_____

_____

_____

_____

_____

4. Who is someone in your life that could benefit from love today? What is something you can do that would be meaningful to them?

_____

_____

_____

_____

_____

NOTES

CHAPTER 3

Respect Boundaries

"Boundaries define us. They define what is me and what is not me. A boundary shows me where I end and someone else begins..."

–Henry Cloud & John Townsend[1]

Most people agree that maintaining and respecting boundaries is essential for a healthy relationship. Boundaries are the rules and limits we establish for ourselves within a relationship. They function like a fence around a piece of property, protecting it from unwanted intruders while also allowing welcome guests inside. Similarly, good boundaries shield an individual from others while fostering intimacy and close relationships.

"Green flag" people respect the boundaries of others. In my experience, it is difficult to honor the boundaries of others when you do not know or respect your own boundaries.

As a young adult, my main struggle was with boundaries. There was a pattern of "people pleasing" that made the maintenance of boundaries difficult. As a "people pleaser" I cared more about the needs of others, their desires, their opinions, and their approval than my own. Conflict was avoided like the plague. *I did not know how to assert what*

GREEN FLAGS

I really wanted or what I was uncomfortable with.

The worst thing about being a "people pleaser" and not having well-defined boundaries is the resentment, burnout, and a lack of personal identity. Without proper boundaries it is hard to know who you are.

Not only did I struggle with knowing my own boundaries, now, I realize I was not always the most respectful of other people's boundaries. There is still some shame in acknowledging this and writing about it in a public manner.

When my marriage was failing and I was battled with deep discontentment, I began flirting and projecting sexual energy that likely crossed the boundaries of my married female friends and co-workers. Reflecting on my actions, I feel remorse for how I must have made some of these women feel. To be fair, I do not believe I was fully aware of these unhealthy patterns at the time.

After working through this in my own therapy, I came to understand that my disregard for other women's boundaries stemmed from a failure to respect my own. Specifically, my inability to confront the frustrations within my marriage led me to seek fulfillment of my erotic needs in inappropriate ways.

Struggles with boundaries is one of the common issues I see in my therapy practice.

CHAPTER 3

Kevin was in his early forties. He was married with two high school aged children. He came to therapy to help save his marriage. He was presently separated from his wife of twenty years. Besides seeing me for individual counseling, he was also working with a couple's therapist.

Kevin came to me saying that he wanted help overcoming his "nice guy syndrome." At the time, it was unclear what he meant by that. After getting to know him a bit, I realized he was referencing the book *No More Mr. Nice Guy* by psychotherapist Robert Glover.

It was easy for me to see my own struggles in Kevin's situation. What he called the "nice guy syndrome" was really a lack of clear boundaries in his marriage. He lacked a real sense of who he was and what he really wanted.

He reported how difficult it was for him to stand up in his marriage and communicate what he really wanted and what was not ok with him. He wanted more frequent sexual intercourse, but struggled to express this out of fear of rejection. He did not like when his wife poked fun at his weight, but could not muster the courage to tell her. His battle with assertiveness was leaving him resentful and bitter.

Kevin's lack of boundaries also led to him not respecting the boundaries of his wife. She loved traveling with her girlfriends and having hobbies that did not involve her husband. Kevin struggled with his wife's independence and would sulk anytime she brought up a weekend away with her friends. Kevin's fragile identity due to lack of clear boundaries, was resulting in co-dependent behavior.

Our work in therapy focused on establishing clear boundaries and growing in assertiveness. I shared with Kevin something I learned from psychotherapist Walter Matweychuk by asking him what he thought about the life philosophy of *putting himself first and others a close second*.[2]

> **SHIFTING FROM TRYING TO PLEASE OTHERS TO FOCUSING ON HIMSELF WOULD ENABLE HIM TO DEVELOP THE STRENGTH NECESSARY TO RELATE HEALTHILY TO HIS WIFE AND OTHERS.**

His initial reaction was not positive. Kevin believed the philosophy seemed selfish and went against his religious conviction that he should serve others before himself. Instead of arguing with him, I suggested he read Matthew McConaughey's book *Greenlights*. I knew McConaughey was one of Kevin's favorite actors.

In *Greenlights*, McConaughey develops a philosophy he calls "egotistical utilitarianism."[3] The egotistical aspect underscores the importance of prioritizing oneself, while the utilitarian aspect empha-

CHAPTER 3

sizes considering the good of others. McConaughey's philosophy aligns with what Matweychuk terms "enlightened self-interest."[4] Flight attendants often remind us that we need to put our oxygen mask on first before putting it on others.

Kevin needed to recognize his genuine needs and desires. *Shifting from trying to please others to focusing on himself would enable him to develop the strength necessary to relate healthily to his wife and others.*

Kevin began practicing this philosophy by going to the movie theater alone, something he once avoided because no one else in his family liked horror movies. He also communicated to his wife that her comments about his weight were unacceptable. Over time, Kevin started going to the gym and adopted a healthier diet. He and his wife eventually reconciled, becoming more intimate than ever. His wife grew very attracted to his newfound confidence and independence.

"Green flag" people respect the boundaries of others because they have learned to respect their own. A philosophy of "egotistical utilitarianism" is crucial to live by if we are going to be the best version of ourselves for others.

Tools for Practice

> **Maintaining Boundaries by Saying "No"**
>
> A great way to clarify and reinforce your boundaries is to practice saying "no." When you say "no," you are promoting self-respect. If someone asks you to do something that makes you feel uncomfortable, saying "no" demonstrates self-awareness.

Saying "no" also helps prevent feelings of resentment. By clearly communicating your boundaries by saying "no," you prevent the buildup of resentment that can happen when you agree to things you do not want. Saying "no" leads to honest and healthy relationships.

Practice saying "no" this week and journal what it was like to express a boundary.

Questions for Discussion

1. What is your definition of a boundary?

_____
_____
_____
_____
_____
_____

CHAPTER 3

2. How are you at having and communicating your boundaries with others?

_____
_____
_____
_____
_____
_____

3. What do you think of the philosophy of "egotistical utilitarianism"?

_____
_____
_____
_____
_____
_____

4. Why is it important to learn how to put ourselves first and others a close second?

_____
_____
_____
_____
_____

NOTES

CHAPTER 4

Manage Your Anxiety

"Anxiety is love's greatest killer. It makes others feel as you might when a drowning man holds on to you. You want to save him, but you know he will strangle you with his panic."

–Anaïs Nin[1]

"Green flag" people leave us feeling energized rather than depleted. One of the greatest markers of a "green flag" person is their commitment to manage their own anxiety.

At one level, anxiety is one of the most human things about us. From an evolutionary perspective, anxiety evolved as a crucial mechanism to protect us from potential threats. Anxiety is connected to our "fight or flight response," priming our bodies to either confront the danger or run away from it. Anxiety has been essential for human survival, aiding our ancestors avoid predators and other life-threatening situations.[2]

If it was not for anxiety, we as a species might not exist. So, anxiety as a feeling of fear, dread and uneasiness is not inherently problematic. Anxiety becomes a real problem when it takes over the command center of our mental functioning. The Pixar movie *Inside Out 2*, illustrates the dangers of anxiety taking over an individual's life.

In the movie, a pubescent Riley begins to encounter new, complex emotions. One of these is Anxiety, which eventually takes control of Riley's emotional command center in an attempt to prevent her from losing social status with her new friends. While anxiety plays a crucial role in our emotional lives, it can cause significant disruption when it dominates.

When helping individuals on managing their anxiety, the analogy from Elizabeth Gilbert's book *Big Magic: Creative Living Beyond Fear* is helpful. Gilbert likens her life to a long road trip, where anxiety is one of the passengers. She acknowledges anxiety's presence and even gives it a seat and a voice on the journey. However, she firmly insists that anxiety is not allowed to take control of the wheel and drive.[3]

I have not always managed my anxiety. There have been times when anxiety was at the wheel directing the course of my life. Instead of trying to contain my anxiety, I would allow it to spill into my relationships.

Before my freshman year of college, I worked as a counselor for a Christian camp in California. After a long day of work, all the counselors would hang out in one of the cabins. Most people would watch TV, play board games or just casually chat. I had an intensity about me that I now recognize was fueled by underlying anxiety about my future.

CHAPTER 4

Instead of decompressing with my co-workers, I wanted to talk about my fears related to college, deeper theological issues, and other personal struggles. I did not pick up the social cues that everyone else wanted to relax and just have a good time. Over a period of weeks, people stopped talking to me and even cut me out of their social gatherings. The result was hurt and insecurity. Looking back, I realize that my anxiety over the future and my faith were draining everyone else who just wanted to enjoy the present moment.

We all know people who are a hive of nerves. Their intensity drains us and leaves us feeling empty. Anaïs Nin is correct that *anxiety is a relationship killer.*

Donovan started therapy to help address his loneliness. He was in his early thirties and a successful mechanical engineer. He desperately wanted a long-term partner. Going on many first dates with men he matched up with on dating apps, he would even extend the relationship beyond the one night to weeks, but eventually something would happen, and the relationship would deteriorate.

Donovan's energy was difficult to be around. He spoke very quickly and would get very passionate about certain subjects he was interested in. His tendency was to talk over me and I experienced that it was difficult for him to establish a mutual relationship with me.

GREEN FLAGS

Donovan was a likable person. He was attractive, had a great sense of style, and was wicked smart. The problem was that his intensity was overwhelming and left me more drained than usual after every session.

During one of his passionate rants, I was compelled to press pause on Donovan and asked him if I could make an observation. He signaled that it was fine for me to do so:

Donovan, you know how much I like you. I think we really have a special connection.

Donovan responded, "Yeah. I like you much better than some of the other therapists I've seen."

"I want to make an observation about something I've noticed. Something that might be playing a role in your struggle to keep a relationship."

"Oh. Ok. Go on," Donovan allowed.

"I think you're really struggling with anxiety and not really managing it well. What you keep calling your 'passion' and 'intensity' may be underlying anxiety that you're not aware of or treating."

Donovan questioned, I'm not sure I understand. I told you I was a passionate dude and a lot of friends appreciate my intensity. I thought you understood that about me?"

CHAPTER 4

"GREEN FLAG" PEOPLE PRIORITIZE MANAGING THEIR ANXIETY, SO THEY ARE NOT DRAINING THEIR RELATIONSHIPS.

"I do. I really admire how passionate you are about the things that matter most to you. I hesitated to say what I did because I would never want to squelch your personality. That said, I feel like part of my role in your life is to help you see the things you cannot see in yourself. While I cherish our relationship, our time together leaves me more depleted than usual. I've been wondering if the men you've dated end up feeling the same as me and if this isn't one of the reasons they end things with you," I responded.

Donovan replied, "So what are you implying! Am I too much for you to handle? Are you going to break it off with me too?"

"No, of course not! I'm committed to you as long as you're wanting to keep this therapeutic relationship. But I do think it's important for us to start addressing your anxiety," I assured him.

Donovan and I started working on his anxiety. Without changing his passion or convictions, we worked on the level of his intensity. As he better managed his anxiety, he started to listen closer, and our relationship felt much more like a mutual exchange than something one-sided. After some time, I no longer felt drained after my time with Donovan.

We ended therapy when Donovan reached his one-year anniversary with Jacob. I was extremely proud of Donovan for managing his anxiety without losing his authentic self.

"Green flag" people prioritize managing their anxiety, so they are not draining their relationships. Like Donovan, it's possible to come to a greater awareness of what is lurking under the surface and to work with it in a way that enhances rather than harms your relationships.

Tools for Practice

Managing Anxiety Through Journaling

Journaling can be an effective tool to help manage anxiety.[4] Journaling can help you:

1. *Express Your Emotions*

Journaling is cathartic. It helps you express negative feelings in a safe, confidential space. Writing down your fears and frustrations can offer a much-needed sense of release.

2. *Gain Insight and Clarity*

CHAPTER 4

Journaling helps you identify your anxiety triggers. It also clarifies patterns of anxiety over a period of time. The more you understand your anxiety, the better equipped you will be to manage it.

3. Problem Solve

Journaling can help you explore solutions to the problems that result in anxiety. Developing a realistic action plan can reduce feelings of helplessness and despair.

Set aside five to fifteen minutes a day to journal about your anxiety. Choose a quiet spot that can help reinforce this activity as a positive habit. Go back to your journal entries throughout the week to track your progress.

Questions for Discussion

1. How do you define anxiety?

_____
_____
_____
_____
_____

2. What is your specific relationship to anxiety?

_____
_____

_____
_____
_____
_____
_____

3. Has your anxiety ever ruined a relationship with someone? If so, how?

_____
_____
_____
_____
_____
_____

4. What did you think of Elizabeth Gilbert's analogy about anxiety as the passenger and not letting it take control? What would it look like to put that into practice in your life?

_____
_____
_____
_____
_____

CHAPTER 5

Listen Without Being Defensive

"Hold your beliefs lightly. Certainty is not necessarily a friend of sanity, although it is often mistaken for it."

–Philippa Perry[1]

"Green flag" people can listen to others without becoming defensive. They can do this because they do not take things too personally. *To not take things so personally, you must hold your opinions, ideas, and beliefs lightly.*

This was a challenge for me in my twenties. As a Christian and pastor, my beliefs were indistinguishable from my identity. In other words, what I thought and what I had faith in, *was who I was*. If my ideas were threatened, my sense of identity was similarly in jeopardy.

This led to a pattern of avoiding interaction with friends and family who might have different views than my own. I was afraid our conversations would instigate doubt, and this would lead to me questioning my position in life.

When my faith was shaken, my whole identity collapsed. I was so closely identified with my Christian beliefs that losing them resulted in a loss of a sense of self. For a few years after, I battled a dark depression. A large part of that experience was navigating life without a clear sense of my identity apart from my beliefs.

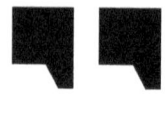

> **GENUINE LISTENING REQUIRES THAT WE LET GO OF OUR NEED TO CONTROL AND OPEN OURSELVES TO THE INFLUENCE OF ANOTHER PERSON.**

When we hold our opinions, ideas, and beliefs too tightly, we have a difficult time listening to other people. *Genuine listening requires that we let go of our need to control and open ourselves to the influence of another person.*

I have a friend who feels compelled to comment on every political social media post he disagrees with. Whether it is someone he knows or not, he will spend a great deal of time explaining why he thinks the person is mistaken. He has told me that he takes any rival political stance as a grave personal offense. *He is so convinced that he is right, he sees his online political activism as a sacred duty.*

I respect my friend's enthusiasm for what he believes is the truth, and understand that he sees his political opinions as life and death matters at times. While never wanting to change his mind, I worry that his extreme commitment to his ideas is blinding

CHAPTER 5

him from other important aspects of life. It comes as no surprise that he has not been successful with any of his romantic relationships.

Relationships require a delicate balance of shared values and respect for differences. My friend states that he values diversity, but has a difficult time honoring the different opinions of people in his life. He cannot seem to find a point of compromise that works for everyone.

Listening to someone without becoming defensive is not the same as agreeing with them. In the therapy office, the practice of defenseless listening helps me nurture my client relationships. My clients are religiously, politically and culturally diverse. Some of them have voted in ways I disagree with. Others believe things I find difficult to accept. None of our differences prevent me from listening to them.

I can listen deeply without getting defensive because I no longer conflate my opinions or beliefs with my identity and worth.

The least enjoyable aspect of any conversation is when people interrupt me or talk over me because their commitment to their opinions supersedes a deeper appreciation for mutual respect and civility. My tendency is to avoid people like that as much as possible.

"Green flag" people listen without becoming defensive because they have put in the work to hold their ideas and beliefs in a humble and flexible posture. By holding their views lightly, they can listen to someone who is different from them and not take any personal offense.

Tools for Practice

> **Taking Things Less Personally by Developing Cognitive Flexibility**
>
> Cognitive flexibility refers to our ability to shift perspectives and adjust our thinking in the face of changing demands.[2] There are several ways to develop cognitive flexibility.

1. *Challenging Assumptions*

Find time to regularly question your own assumptions and beliefs. Ask yourself questions like, "Why do I believe this?" or "Are there alternative viewpoints?"

2. *Perspective Taking*

Try to adopt the perspective of a friend or family member you disagree with. Seek to understand the reasoning behind their opinions. Resist the urge to defend your own views.

3. *Expose Yourself to Diverse Views*

CHAPTER 5

Read books and watch documentaries that present viewpoints that differ from your own. Exposure to different perspectives helps you see the complexity of issues. Often, there are multiple valid perspectives.

Questions for Discussion

1. Are there any opinions, views, or beliefs that you are holding in too strong a manner?

2. Are you capable of listening to someone you really disagree with without getting defensive? If not, why is that?

3. Do you know someone like my friend in this chapter? Have you ever talked to them about their problematic behavior?

4. Pick an important point in your belief system. What would it look like to hold that view in a more flexible way?

CHAPTER 6

Let Others Be Themselves

"If I have lost confidence in myself, I have the universe against me."

–Ralph Waldo Emerson[1]

"Green flag" people let others be themselves because they are confident in who they are. When you are confident in yourself, you are comfortable with other people's differences.

Much of what I do in therapy is help individuals grow in confidence. I like to explain the word confidence comes from the Latin "*con*" (with) and "*fidere*" (trust). *The confident person is the one who has faith or trust in their abilities and direction in life.*

Confidence is walking into a room and believing you are good enough. Not any better, and surely not any worse. Confidence allows you to stand eye to eye with others.

Many of the couples I see in therapy struggle with confidence in their relationship. One person in the relationship feels the need to change the other person. A husband wants his wife to stay at home and not go back to school. A girlfriend is threatened by her boyfriend's interest in a religion that is not her own. A lack of confidence can lead to an increasing need to control perceived threats to the individual.

Anytime I see a person trying to change or control another, I look for the underlying insecurity and how I can help them develop confidence.

Beth and Roger came to see me to improve communication in their relationship. They had been married sixteen years and had three beautiful children together. There was clearly deep love and commitment in their marriage.

Lately, the couple had been caught in a negative cycle of frustration and blame. When they first got married, the two of them agreed that Roger would build his career as an architect and Beth would stay at home and raise the kids. Now that the kids were older, Beth felt a pull to go back to school and get her master's degree in psychology. One of their children was autistic, and Beth had spent countless hours seeking to understand the diagnosis. In the process of supporting her child, she developed a strong interest in psychology and found herself fantasying about becoming a therapist herself.

It was obvious that Roger was not pleased with this recent development. When Beth would bring up the desire to go back to school, Roger would get flooded with negative emotions and either storm out of the room or respond with something hurtful he later regretted.

CHAPTER 6

At first, I wrongly assumed Roger was stuck on a traditional mindset and did not want his wife back in the workforce. When I realized that was not the issue, I guessed again, he worried that his wife being in school would create greater responsibilities for him at home. But this too was not the case. On an intellectual level, Roger believed in the equality of women and was happy to help more with the kids. In fact, he was at a point in his career where he had great flexibility to assist his wife with driving the children to different activities after school.

> **ADDRESSING YOUR INSECURITIES AND BUILDING YOUR CONFIDENCE CAN HELP YOU BECOME A PERSON THAT ALLOWS OTHERS TO BE EXACTLY WHO THEY ARE.**

I was confused about Roger's negative reaction to his wife's desire to further her education. On paper, he not only had zero issues with it, but he even encouraged it. *There must have been an unconscious conflict that was contributing to his negative outbursts.*

After learning more about Roger's struggles with his career, it became clear to me why he was so bothered by his wife's excitement about the prospect of going back to school. Roger was a partner at a successful architecture firm. At this stage, he spent the bulk of his time managing people instead of doing the actual work of architecture. Until his time in therapy, he had not articulated the sadness he felt in being disconnected from the creative work he once loved.

Roger's emotional outbursts were less about his wife's excitement and more informed by his own lack of confidence and purpose at work. It became apparent that his wife's passion for something new and exciting reminded him of how much he dreaded his current role.

I suggested that Roger think about how he could reconnect with the creative work that truly energized him. After some reflection, Roger decided to have a conversation with the other partners. They decided that he could focus on more creative ventures as long as he did not lose sight of some of his managerial responsibilities. Roger agreed to the new arrangement.

This reconnection with his confidence and passion resolved his frustration with his wife. He was finally able to encourage her to pursue her dreams.

Addressing your insecurities and building your confidence can help you become a person that allows others to be exactly who they are.

CHAPTER 6

Tools for Practice

> **Building Confidence Through Physical Exercise**
>
> One of the best ways to build confidence is to start a regular physical exercise routine. Exercise boosts endorphins, reduces stress and improves your overall sense of well-being.

Commit to starting a morning workout routine. Here are a few ideas to help you get started.

1. *Prepare The Night Before*

Lay out your workout clothes and shoes to reduce the morning friction.

2. *Consistent Wake-Up Time*

Commit to waking up at the same time. This will help regulate your body's internal clock and help this become a sustainable habit.

3. *Variety of Exercises*

Change up what you do to keep things interesting. Try running, yoga, cycling or lifting weights.

4. *Listen to Podcasts or Audiobooks*

Use this time to sharpen your mind. There are plenty of podcasts and audiobooks that are designed to help you grow in confidence.

Questions for Discussion

1. How do you define confidence?

___

2. Are there any ways you struggle with confidence in your relationships?

___

3. Has there been a time you struggled to encourage a loved one because of a lack of confidence?

___

CHAPTER 6

_____

_____

4. What is something you could do that would help you feel greater confidence?

_____

_____

_____

_____

_____

_____

NOTES

CHAPTER 7

Help People Feel Safe

"Trust is the glue of life. It's the most essential ingredient in effective communication. It's the foundational principle that holds all relationships."

–Steven Covey[1]

As humans, we feel safe in relationships when we believe that we can trust the other person and believe they have honesty, integrity, and loyalty. *The bedrock of trust is honesty.* If you cannot be honest with yourself and others, you will not be capable of healthy relationships.

Honesty leads to a feeling of safety in relationship because it fosters an environment of dependability. Most of us crave order and consistency. When we do not have those things, we begin to feel insecure and unstable, and therefore feel unsafe.

When a friend tells me he will call me in two hours, I feel confused when the call fails to arrive. When your child tells you they completed the task you asked them to accomplish, you feel upset when you discover it was a lie. The negative reaction stems from your deep need for trustworthiness. If we cannot trust our loved ones, the world becomes a scary and unpredictable place.

GREEN FLAGS

Christopher was a sixteen-year-old boy who started therapy with me at his parent's request. Like most young men who are forced into therapy, Christopher was initially resistant. After a few sessions, I was able to connect with him and establish a strong therapeutic bond.

Christopher's parents were furious he had lied to them about smoking marijuana. This was something that went against the religious values of the family. But, for the parents, worse than smoking was the betrayal. They had trusted Christopher, and he deceived them.

At first, Christopher did not seem to care about hurting his parents. He was far more interested in spending time with his friends and having a good time. He deemed smoking as harmless and declared he would go back to it the moment his parents ungrounded him.

Nothing I said about the virtues of truth and honesty stuck with Christopher. He agreed with me at a theoretical level, but clearly was not emotionally invested enough to change his behavior.

Not until he got a taste of his own medicine. A few months into our therapy, Christopher started talking to a teenage girl at his school. It was obvious that Christopher was smitten with Claire. He spent a large amount of our sessions pining over her and describing how much he loved their relationship.

CHAPTER 7

One morning, Christopher walked into my office with tears in his eyes. He sat down and completely broke down. Trying to honor the moment, I gave him all the time he needed to express his sadness. This was the first time I witnessed this level of emotional expression from Christopher before this session.

He eventually explained that Claire had cheated on him with his best friend. A double betrayal. He was devastated. He had lost his appetite and was having a hard time sleeping.

When we were at a point to finally process what happened, Christopher explained that he felt like he would never be able to trust anyone again. His world felt upside down, and he never wanted to put himself in a situation to feel like that again.

I comforted him and assured him that he would get through this. It would take time, but his heart would eventually heal, and he would be capable of loving again.

As difficult as it was for me to go there, I asked if we could stay close to the pain of betrayal. At first, he was upset and wondered why I would encourage him to do that. I told him that sometimes the only way we learn is through our own intense suffering.

We journeyed together through the trauma and grief of the betrayal. After a few months, he started to regain some of his spunk and personality. I will never forget what he told me one session:

> **"GREEN FLAG" PEOPLE PRIORITIZE HONESTY AND TRUSTWORTHINESS. THIS IS ESSENTIAL TO ENSURING OTHERS FEEL SAFE AND SECURE IN A RELATIONSHIP WITH YOU.**

"I hate that my girlfriend cheated on me with my best friend. That was the worst thing that has ever happened to me. I know I'm still not fully over it. I've now got trust issues that I'll have to navigate for years."

I replied, "Yeah, man. That was awful. But I sense you're wanting to say something else about it."

Christopher was thoughtful. "I would never wish what happened to me on my worst enemy," he said. "But I don't think I would have realized how important being honest and trustworthy is if that hadn't happened to me."

Christopher was able to have an honest conversation with his parents. He told them he disagreed with their value of no drugs in the house. He was clear that once he was living on his own, he would start smoking again. But in the meantime, he would respect their rules and prioritize being honest with them.

"Green flag" people prioritize honesty and trustworthiness. This is essential to ensuring others feel safe and secure in a relationship with you.

> **Maintaining Honesty Through "Rituals of Connection"** [2]
>
> Frequent connection with our partners encourages honest conversation. Schedule bi-weekly times to discuss your feelings, thoughts and experiences with your partner. These "rituals of connection" can include brief conversations, evening routines, date nights and vacations.

Tools for Practice:

An Example of an Evening Ritual of Connection

My wife and I sit in our breakfast nook several times a week. We set aside our phones and commit to having an uninterrupted conversation. We typically enjoy a nice cocktail together. We take this time to discuss the highs and lows of our day. If there is something difficult we need to tell the other person, we do it during this time.

This recurring ritual of connection encourages us to maintain honesty in the relationship.

Questions for Discussion:

1. What do you believe is the function of hones-

ty in a relationship?

_____
_____
_____
_____
_____
_____

2. Can you think of a time you were not honest with a friend or partner? What was the larger impact?

_____
_____
_____
_____
_____
_____

3. Have you ever been betrayed? If so, what was something you learned about yourself through the process?

_____
_____
_____
_____
_____
_____

4. Is there something you've been struggling to share with a loved one? What would be the benefits

CHAPTER 7

of coming clean to them?

NOTES

CHAPTER 8

Don't Project unto Others

"Do not judge, or you too will be judged."

–Jesus[1]

The most refreshing people in my life are those that do not police my speech or behavior. I enjoy the feeling of being myself, warts and all. I do not appreciate people that need me to speak or act differently in order to be their friend.

Early into my conversion to Christianity, I developed a friendship with someone who needed to be the enforcer of my behavior. Like most teenage boys, I enjoyed swearing and making outlandish jokes. Once, this person pulled me aside and had a very serious conversation with me. He told me that my coarse language was offensive to him and to God. I felt humiliated and ashamed. From that point on, I tried to edit what I said and did around him. It was exhausting and felt disingenuous.

Over a decade later, after our friendship had dissolved, it became clear to me why this person needed to police me and those around him. As I immersed myself in the writings of Carl Jung, I discovered the concept of *projection*.[2] To put it simply, *we tend to see in other people what we have not accepted in ourselves.*

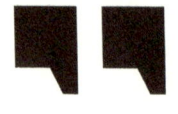

> **"GREEN FLAG" PEOPLE DO THE HARD WORK TO IDENTIFY AND MANAGE THE PARTS OF THEMSELVES THAT ARE DIFFICULT TO INTEGRATE INTO A BALANCED PERSONALITY.**

There was a time we went to the movie theater and during a scene with nudity, he covered my eyes for a few seconds. It would later come out he had a serious addiction to pornography. He tried to shield my eyes from the woman's breast because he could not acknowledge his own complicated relationship with sexual desire.

Jesus said that before we can pull the speck of dust out of our neighbor's eye, we must remove the log from our own eye.[3] Instead of trying to regulate the actions and speech of others, we should learn to accept the difficult aspects of ourselves.

Carl Rogers[4] believed that unconditional positive regard is an essential element of effective psychotherapy. Unconditional positive regard is acceptance and support of another, regardless of what they say or do. "Green flag" people practice unconditional positive regard in their relationship with others.

CHAPTER 8

Over the last year, one of my teenage sons has developed moral views that are quite different than my own. We often get into heated disagreements. Immature parts of me want to lecture him on why he's wrong and threaten him with a punishment if he doesn't change his mind. When I can take a step back and practice unconditional positive regard, I can disagree with him without the need to control or reject him. I can treat him with love and respect even when we do not see eye to eye.

"Green flag" people do the hard work to identify and manage the parts of themselves that are difficult to integrate into a balanced personality. They understand they can relate to others with love and acceptance, even if they do not agree or condone their lifestyle and values.

Tools for Practice

> **Withdrawing Projections by Tracking Strong Emotional Reactions**
>
> In the story *Demian*, Hermann Hesse writes, "If you hate a person, you hate something in him that is part of yourself."[5] But what if instead of self-hatred, you learned to embrace all that you are?

As you develop a journaling practice, start to track strong emotional reactions you experience around other people. If you are enraged by certain things, it is possible these are qualities in yourself that have not yet been brought to conscious awareness. By noticing these responses, even the ones you perceive as negative, you are learning to love and accept yourself more fully and therefore love and accept others.

Talk to a friend or therapist about these patterns of strong emotional reaction. Another person may be able to see something in you that you cannot see all by yourself.

Questions for Discussion

1. What does Carl Jung's understanding of projection say about us in relation to judging others?

___

2. What is a darker part of you that has been difficult to integrate into your larger personality?

___

CHAPTER 8

3. Think of a person in your life that you are quick to judge. What within you must be addressed first before you could address anything about them?

_____
_____
_____
_____
_____
_____

4. How might you apply Carl Roger's notion of unconditional positive regard to your relationships?

_____
_____
_____
_____
_____
_____

NOTES

CHAPTER 9

Support Others' Goals

"As you navigate through the rest of your life, be open to collaboration. Other people and other people's ideas are often better than your own. Find a group of people who challenge and inspire you, spend a lot of time with them, and it will change your life."

—Amy Poehler[1]

"Green flag" people support the goals of others. To support the dreams of others, you first must be content and secure in your own life and plans. *I have found those who are most competitive in interpersonal relationships tend to be the most insecure in their own sense of worth and value.* I say that in part because that is how I used to be.

During my vocation as a pastor, I was struck by low self-esteem and a deep sense of inadequacy. None of the work that I have encouraged in this book was something I practiced.

In one of my positions, I worked with another pastor who was ten years my senior. He was a good person and always kind to me. Regardless of our positive relationship, my self-doubt and insecurities emerged anytime I was around him. I often compared myself to him. Anytime he connected with someone or preached a sermon, I became envious of his abilities. Most of the time, I imagined that he was a much better pastor than I could ever be.

My client Theresa came to see me to help address her depression. She had recently broken up with a long-term boyfriend and was trying to figure out what she was going to do after trade school. Her friend, Jennifer, would invite her to run errands on the weekends. Jennifer thought getting Theresa out of her dark room and into the sunlight would be good for her mood. Jennifer had recently started a job as a veterinarian technician. She also started a workout routine at the gym and was beginning to lose weight. She was on multiple dating applications and was busy going on first dates.

Theresa appreciated her friend's support but was threatened by her apparent success. During one session, Theresa asked me:

"Why do I feel like I am in competition with my friend? Every time I'm around her, I feel like I have to compare myself to her. I look at her life and I realize she has all the things I wish I had."

Empathizing with Theresa, I told her it must be hard to feel like she was in competition with one of her best friends. At the same time, my encouragement was for her to stay close to her negative emotions and get curious about what they could teach her.

We discovered that her need to compare herself to Jennifer had less to do with Jennifer's success and more with her own dissatisfaction with her life. Anytime she felt the need to compare herself, she could pause and ask herself what in her life she would like to improve. After several weeks of doing this, Theresa concluded that she wanted to figure out what she was going to do for a career. She also desired to get in better shape so she could feel more confident in dating.

> **"GREEN FLAG" PEOPLE DO THE HARD WORK TO IDENTIFY AND MANAGE THE PARTS OF THEMSELVES THAT ARE DIFFICULT TO INTEGRATE INTO A BALANCED PERSONALITY.**

I belong to an informal group called the "Diamond Dogs," after the group of men who support each other on the TV show *Ted Lasso*. We four come from different cultural, religious and political backgrounds. Our group chat is a place to encourage and inspire one another. We share book recommendations, jokes, recipes and other random things, anything that might pique interest. It is a space to share whatever good is happening in our lives, as well as the moments of disappointment and sadness.

I could not have been in a group like this ten years ago. At the time, comparison and competition would have overwhelmed me. Now I rejoice in our diversity and try to see their successes as a chance to celebrate them and challenge myself.

"Green flag" people can support the goals of

others because they are secure in their life. Collaboration and healthy competition are sought after instead of feared when you have done the work to address your deeper insecurities.

Tools for Practice

> **Support Yourself and Others in Community**
>
> Finding a supportive community can be a great asset in your life. This does not have to be a traditional church or religious group. You want to find a community that aligns with your values. It is important this community can simultaneously encourage and challenge you.

If a community like this does not exist around you, create one. You can even build a community online.

Questions for Discussion

1. Talk about how you support the goals of others. What might make this difficult?

___
___
___
___
___

CHAPTER 9

2. Who in your life is thriving? What can you learn about their apparent success?

3. What is your involvement in a supportive community? If there isn't one, what would be some of the benefits of being a part of something like that?

4. Think of someone important in your life? What is something great they have recently accomplished that you can acknowledge?

NOTES

CONCLUSION

Continuing to Bring Forth What is Within

"The paradox of individuation is that we best serve intimate relationship by becoming sufficiently developed in ourselves that we do not need to feed off others."

-James Hollis[1]

The greatest gift we can give our family and friends is putting in the work to become the best possible version of ourselves. I have argued that we become our best self when *we seek to make what is unconscious conscious in our life.*

In The Gospel of Thomas, Jesus says, "If you bring forth what is within you, what you bring forth will save you. If you do not bring forth what is within you, what you do not bring forth will destroy you."[2]

Understood from a depth psychological perspective, *Jesus is highlighting the dangers of letting your negative unconscious patterns govern your life.* The only way to have a healthy relationship is to bring forth our inner demons and refuse to let them drive us and our relationships into the ground. We must also bring forward what is compelling us to achieve our dreams and desires. Denying these realities can mean the difference between salvation and destruction, life and death.

> **WHATEVER PATH YOU CHOOSE, I HOPE YOU CAN FIND THE COURAGE TO CONFRONT THE DARKER PARTS OF YOURSELF TO LIGHT THE WAY FOR A BRIGHTER FUTURE.**

There is no one right way to make the unconscious conscious. If being a "green flag" person is a goal for you, then there is a way to reach it. Many choose the path of psychotherapy or psychoanalysis. If this is for you, my encouragement is to reach out to me or a therapist who might be the right person to guide you toward being the person you want to be.

This path worked for me and even saved my life. For others, a trusted friend or mentor can do the trick. I know people whose romantic partner serves as the mirror that helps them come to terms with their destructive unconscious patterns.

Whatever path you choose, I hope you can find the courage to confront the darker parts of yourself to light the way for a brighter future.

ENDNOTES

Introduction
1 Hollis, J. (1998). *The Eden project: In search of the magical other* (p. 19). Toronto, Canada: Inner City Books.
2 Aurelius, M. (2002). *Meditations* (G. Hays, Trans.). Modern Library. p. 144.
3 Holiday, R. (2016). *The daily Stoic: 366 meditations on wisdom, perseverance, and the art of living* (p. 27). New York, NY: Portfolio.
4 Depth psychology focuses on the unconscious aspects of the human psyche, exploring how hidden motivations, feelings, and experiences influence behavior and personality. It encompasses theories and practices from prominent figures like Sigmund Freud, Carl Jung, and their followers, emphasizing the importance of dreams, symbols, and archetypes in understanding the human mind. For a comprehensive overview, see Carl Gustav Jung's The Undiscovered Self (1957).
5 *Instagram.* (Feb 6th, 2024). "Green Flags" [Instagram post]. Retrieved July 28, 2024, https://www.

instagram.com/herpsychology/

Chapter 1

1 Larson, C. D. (1910). *Your forces and how to use them*. Retrieved from https://www.craftdeology.com/inspiring-poem-promise-yourself-by-christian-d-larson/.

2 Autism spectrum disorder (ASD) is a developmental disorder characterized by difficulties with social interaction, communication challenges, and a tendency to engage in repetitive behaviors. The severity and combination of symptoms vary widely among individuals. Diagnosis is typically based on a comprehensive evaluation of behavior and development.

3 Neurotypical is a term used to describe individuals whose neurological development and functioning are considered typical or within the expected range. Neurotypical people do not exhibit the characteristics of neurodevelopment disorders such as autism, ADHD, or other cognitive variations.

4 Peck, M. S. (1978). *The road less traveled: A new psychology of love, traditional values, and spiritual growth* (p. 32). New York, NY: Simon & Schuster.

5 Brown, B. (2012). Daring greatly: How the courage to be vulnerable transforms the way we live, love, parent, and lead (p. 69). Gotham Books.

6 Kristin Neff's concept of self-compassion involves treating oneself with kindness, recognizing shared humanity, and being mindful of personal suffering. It encourages a positive relationship with oneself to foster emotional resilience and well-being. See

ENDNOTES

Neff, K. (2011). *Self-compassion: The proven power of being kind to yourself*. HarperCollins.

Chapter 2

1 Fromm, E. (1956). *The art of loving* (p. 99). New York, NY: Harper & Row.
2 Narcissistic Personality Disorder (NPD) is a mental condition characterized by an inflated sense of self-importance, a deep need for excessive attention and admiration, troubled relationships, and a lack of empathy for others. Despite this grandiosity, individuals with NPD often have fragile self-esteem and are vulnerable to the slightest criticism.
3 Boothby, R. (2023) *On the subject of love*. Unpublished Manuscript. Department of Philosophy, Loyola University Maryland, Baltimore, Maryland.
4 Brownell, J. (2012). *Listening: Attitudes, principles, and skills* (5th ed.). Pearson.
5 Wayne State University. (n.d.). *Becoming an active listener*. Retrieved from https://wayne.edu/learning-communities/pdf/becoming-active-listener-13.pdf

Chapter 3

1 Cloud, H., & Townsend, J. (1992). *Boundaries: When to say yes, how to say no to take control of your life* (p. 31). Grand Rapids, MI: Zondervan.
2 Matweychuk, W. J. (n.d.). REBT resources and articles. Retrieved from https://www.rebtdoctor.com/
3 Matthew McConaughey discusses the concept of

"egotistical utilitarianism" in his memoir Greenlights. He describes it as the idea where the most selfish decisions one makes for themselves also happen to be the most selfless decisions, benefiting the most people. McConaughey uses this term to explain how self-interest and altruism can align, where personal fulfillment and responsibility to others are interconnected. See McConaughey, M. (2020). *Greenlights*. New York, NY: Crown.

4 Matweychuk, W. J. (2024). *Putting yourself first and others a close second – The philosophy of enlightened self-interest*. Retrieved from https://www.rebtdoctor.com/putting-yourself-first-and-others-a-close-second.html

Chapter 4

1 Nin, A. (1966). *The diary of Anaïs Nin*, Vol. 4: 1944-1947 (p. xx). New York, NY: Harcourt Brace Jovanovich.

2 For a comprehensive exploration of the evolutionary roots of human anxiety, see: Nesse, R. M. (2019). *Good reasons for bad feelings: Insights from the frontier of evolutionary psychiatry*. New York, NY: Dutton. This book delves into how evolutionary perspectives can shed light on various mental health issues, including anxiety, and offers insights into why certain emotional responses have developed as they have.

3 Gilbert, E. (2015). *Big magic: Creative living beyond fear* (pgs. 25-26). New York, NY: Riverhead Books.

4 Bourne, E. J. (2015). *The anxiety and phobia*

workbook (6th ed.). New Harbinger Publications.

Chapter 5

1 Perry, P. (2012). *How to stay sane* (p. 28). New York, NY: Picador.
2 Scott, W. A. (1962). *Cognitive complexity and cognitive flexibility*. In *Human Relations* (pp. 153-176). Harper & Row.

Chapter 6

1 Emerson, R. W. (1941). *The complete writings of Ralph Waldo Emerson* (p. 304). New York, NY: Wm. H. Wise & Co.

Chapter 7

1 Covey, S. R., Merrill, A. R., & Merrill, R. R. (1995). *First things first* (p. 203). New York, NY: Simon & Schuster.
2 These are regular, meaningful activities or routines that couples create together to strengthen their emotional bond and enhance their relationship. See Gottman, J. M., & Silver, N. (1999). *The seven principles for making marriage work*.

Chapter 8

1 *The Holy Bible*, New International Version. (2011). Zondervan. (Original work published ca. A.D. 70, Matthew 7:1).
2 Carl Jung's notion of projection refers to the psychological process where individuals attribute their own unconscious thoughts, feelings, and motivations onto another person. This mechanism allows

people to see qualities in others that they deny or repress in themselves. For more detailed information, you can refer to: Jung, C. G. (1968). *The archetypes and the collective unconscious* (2nd ed.). Princeton University Press.

3 *The Holy Bible*, New International Version. (2011). Zondervan. (Original work published ca. A.D. 70, Matthew 7:3-5).

4 Carl Rogers was a pioneering American psychologist and one of the founders of the humanistic approach to psychology. He developed the client-centered therapy, emphasizing the importance of a supportive, non-judgmental environment to facilitate personal growth and self-discovery. Rogers believed in the inherent goodness and potential of individuals, advocating for empathy, authenticity, and unconditional positive regard in therapeutic settings.

5 Hesse, H. (1923). *Demian: The story of Emil Sinclair's youth* (M. Roloff & M. Lebeck, Trans.). Harper & Row. (Original work published 1919). (p. 182).

Chapter 9
1 Poehler, A. (2014). *Yes please*. New York, NY: Dey Street Books.

Conclusion
1 Hollis, J. (1993). *The middle passage: From misery to meaning in midlife* (p. 99).

2 *Gospel of Thomas*, saying 70. (n.d.). The Nag Hammadi Library in English. Retrieved from [https://www.nag-hammadi.com/gospel-of-thomas].

ACKNOWLEDGEMENTS

I would like to express my deepest gratitude to those who have supported and guided me throughout the journey of creating this book.

To Sean Fitzpatrick and the Jung Center Houston, thank you for providing a healing and creative space during one of the most difficult times in my life. Your center became a sanctuary where I could find solace, inspiration, and the strength to continue.

A special thank you to Phuc Luu for his invaluable guidance and mentorship throughout this process. Without your wisdom and unwavering support, this project would not have been possible. Your insights have shaped this book in profound ways, and I am deeply grateful.

To my friend Patrick McGrath Muñiz, who stood by me during my existential crisis and inspired me to reconnect with my psyche, thank you. Your friendship and guidance have been a beacon of light, and your influence is woven into the very fabric of this book.

I am also profoundly grateful to my beloved "Diamond Dog" group. You have provided a space for me to share my joys, sorrows, and eccentricities without judgment. Your companionship has been a source of strength and comfort, and I cherish each of you.

Lastly, to Aaron Inkrott, a wise friend who took the time to read this book and offered deep encouragement, thank you. Your thoughtful feedback and kind words gave me the confidence to bring this project to completion.

This book is a testament to the power of community, friendship, and the support of those who believe in you. I am forever indebted to all of you.

ABOUT THE AUTHOR

Quique Autrey (LPC, MS, MDiv) is the co-founder and lead therapist at the Neurodiversity Center of Katy. With over two decades of experience, he has been committed to helping individuals uncover and embrace their authentic selves. Through personalized therapy and deep exploration, Quique guides his clients in understanding their true nature and living in alignment with their core values. In addition to his work as a therapist, he also hosts the *Psyche* podcast.